Men in Black

Evidence and True Stories about Earth's Most Mysterious Cover Agents

Conrad Bauer

Copyrights

All rights reserved © 2018 by Conrad Bauer and Maplewood Publishing. No part of this publication or the information in it may be quoted from or reproduced in any form by means such as printing, scanning, photocopying, or otherwise without prior written permission of the copyright holder.

Disclaimer and Terms of Use

Efforts has been made to ensure that the information in this book is accurate and complete. However, the author and the publisher do not warrant the accuracy of the information, text, and graphics contained within the book due to the rapidly changing nature of science, research, known and unknown facts, and internet. The author and the publisher do not hold any responsibility for errors, omissions, or contrary interpretation of the subject matter herein. This book is presented solely for motivational and informational purposes only

ISBN: 978-1720425977

Printed in the United States

Contents

The Strange Persuasion of the Men in Black — 1

Albert Bender's Mind-Bending — 3

Experience with MIB — 3

Contact Day — 9

Bender Tenders his Resignation — 15

The MIB Charade Continues — 21

The Solway Firth Spaceman — 27

Unmasking the Imposters — 31

John Keel Enters into the Mystery — 37

Further Misadventures with the MIB — 45

Silent Witnesses to the MIB — 53

The Infallibility of the MIB — 61

Who Are the MIB? And What Do They Want? — 65

Further Readings — 67

Also by Conrad Bauer — 71

The Strange Persuasion of the Men in Black

They typically come in groups of three, completely unannounced, pounding on the doors of individuals who have somehow been involved with UFOs. As soon as some unlucky person answers the door, these strange figures forcefully barge into his home brandishing official looking badges and shouting incoherently. From the very beginning, these strange men dressed all in black seem intent on creating as much disruption and discord as they possibly can. It's like a bizarre sting operation by an unknown authority, with no immediate purpose except to rattle and disturb the target.

But then, after the hapless host is made a complete wreck by the opening barrage, the MIB change the course of the conversation to aliens and UFOs. If the person recently took a photo of a craft, these strange men seem to know all about it—and they even know details that the photographer never noticed. Once the purpose of their startling apparition is made known, they typically make a vague but completely chilling threat that if their host doesn't "stop talking about UFOs", he is going to regret it.

Besides threatening the person, they sometimes attempt to assure him that his cooperation is for the "good of the country", or at times even for the "good of the world"—and even more strangely, these odd men have occasionally claimed that obeying their commands is "for the good of the universe".

But just what country, world, or indeed universe these strange entities are from remains a complete unknown. At first, it was assumed that the MIB were nothing more than the government agents that they sometimes claimed to be—a secret branch of the Air Force, the CIA, or perhaps even members of the FBI.

But as the strangeness of MIB encounters continued to escalate, it became clear to most experiencers and researchers alike that the entities known as the Men in Black represented something no mere government agency could explain. Upon closer examination, their appearance often seemed startlingly inhuman. Their skin has been reported to look like plastic or rubber, and they allegedly have no hair on their bodies or their heads—not only are they bald and clean-shaven, they don't even have eyebrows! And if they look somewhat like mannequins, their behavior is also often reported to be robotic. They walk and move about in a clumsy fashion, and they also seem to struggle with the basics of normal human interaction, often misusing common words and displaying odd and off-putting body language.

This was very much the case in the very first recorded encounter with the MIB, when a mild-mannered fisherman named Harold A. Dahl had a rather traumatic brush with the unknown. Dahl was aboard his fishing vessel with his son and their dog when he noticed six strange-looking unidentified craft flying overhead. As they stared up at the unusual craft, one of them dumped what Dahl later described as "molten lava" onto their boat. Whether it was intentional or not, this hot metal scored a direct hit on their dog, killing it on the spot. Although their lives were spared, Dahl and his son suffered from severe burns and had to be hospitalized. Dahl was obviously shaken by the experience, but he recuperated, and he even had the presence of mind to collect the slag that had solidified aboard his fishing boat.

Soon after this rare find, Dahl received that dreaded knock on his door and found a man dressed head to toe in black standing before him. The man seemed painfully out of place, and yet at the same time he projected terrifying authority as he demanded that Dahl forget everything he had witnessed. After several such visitations, Dahl was thoroughly convinced. He didn't know who the man was, but he felt compelled to listen to the strange persuasion of the Man in Black.

Albert Bender's Mind-Bending Experience with MIB

Among the first and most well-documented MIB accounts—indeed, the account that perhaps kick-started them all—was the experience of a simple office clerk named Albert Bender. Mr. Bender was an unlikely candidate for the fame and notoriety he would soon acquire. After a brief stint in the military during World War Two, he returned to live in his stepfather's attic. In his early 30's at the time, he was somewhat of a late bloomer and was still struggling to find his way in life.

But from within those humble walls of his stepdad's attic, Bender eventually founded the first major civilian UFO investigation group, the International Flying Saucer Bureau (IFSB). Bender brought the IFSB to the forefront in the search for answers in the nascent UFO phenomenon in April of 1952 with the publication of a periodical called *The Space Review*. Bender's obsession with UFOs stuck a chord, and soon like-minded enthusiasts from around the world were contacting him with their own sightings.

In today's parlance, you could say that Bender's organization and magazine went viral. But as wildly popular as the IFSB became, it wouldn't be long before the organization was completely shut down. Just a few months later, following a visit from none other than the Men in Black, Bender became the subject of a wide array of strange phenomena. The activity began with a simple phone call.

Bender's stepfather was out at the time, so he was alone in the house. It should have been a simple enough matter for him to pick up the old fashioned rotary phone that the two shared, but as soon as he put the phone to his ear, he felt strange. He felt a sudden, inexplicable chill go up and down his spine. And as he repeatedly asked, "Hello? Hello?" no one responded. But even though no response was forthcoming, Bender had the distinct feeling that there was indeed somebody listening to him through the phone.

After a few moments of eerie silence, Bender felt dizzy and slammed the phone down. He headed straight to his bed, where he immediately fell into a fitful sleep. It was an odd occurrence and easily forgotten, but just a little later in the week, the strange phone call returned to Bender's mind in light of another much more inexplicable occurrence. Putting aside the pressures of running the IFSB, Bender was trying to enjoy an evening alone at his local cinema, the place he usually went when he wanted to clear his mind.

The movie—no doubt one of the many B- movie science fiction films that were popular at the time—turned out to be a bust, however, and not much for holding his attention. It was just past midnight when the movie ended and Bender began walking home alone through the sleepy city streets. He was keeping an eye out for muggers, just in case, but it wasn't a robber he had to worry about—it was something much more nebulous that seemed to be pursuing him.

Although he couldn't make out a distinct figure tracing his footsteps in the darkness, he couldn't shake the feeling that something was following him. Feeling like he'd suddenly been cast in his very own horror movie, Bender quickened his steps as he neared the modest home he shared with his stepfather. Upon reaching it he let himself in and quickly shut the door behind him, making sure it was locked up tight. Knowing that his stepdad was already asleep, he then quietly made his way up to his attic room.

When he opened the door he made a startling discovery. First, his nose was assailed with a horrible smell of burning sulfur, and the next thing he knew he was face to face with a floating orb. Orbs have been part and parcel of the paranormal for quite a long time, and it has variously been speculated that these floating, glowing objects are the spirits of the deceased, inter-dimensional entities, or the high-tech surveillance equipment of an extraterrestrial civilization. But all Bender knew was that there was a shining ball of light floating in the middle of his attic bedroom.

Not knowing what else to do, Bender quickly switched on the room's overhead light. As soon as he did so, the orb blinked out of existence as if it was never there in the first place. Were his eyes playing tricks on him? Was it lack of sleep? The product of a worried mind? Bender didn't know what he was dealing with, but as he scanned his room, he began to realize that it most certainly wasn't all in his mind. Whatever it was, this orb had left its calling card in the form of wrecked items all over his attic. All of his files were scattered on the floor, as if they had been perused by someone who was searching through them frantically. Was this connected to the ball of light? How was it that this shining orb had scattered his UFO files all over the place? What was it looking for?

Despite the shock of this experience, Bender, demonstrating calmer nerves than most, was able to put the matter behind him. Temporarily placing speculation on the backburner, he decided to move on with his work of organizing upcoming events and meetings for the IFSB faithful.

He also had time to arrange another trip to the local movie theater, where he took in yet another sci-fi feature in November of 1952. Once again, he encountered something that he could not fully explain, and this time it was inside the theater itself. He was sitting in his seat watching the movie when he had the unmistakable feeling that someone was staring at him. He looked all around him, but he couldn't see anyone in particular looking his way. Aside from the few other moviegoers, there was nothing there but absolute darkness.

But then, as he glanced around, he was shocked to see a man dressed all in black appear out of nowhere and occupy the empty seat next to him. It was like the seat was empty one second, and then the very next, this frightening little man dressed all in black was sitting in it—as if the entity had just popped into existence.

As strange as his arrival was, the way he looked was even stranger. He had all of the trappings of what we have come to describe as the Men in Black. He wore the long black trench coat and the black fedora hat, but much more astonishingly, he also had a pair of eyes that glowed unnaturally in the semi-darkness of the movie theater.

As he had during the strange phone call, and during the previous walk home, Bender felt like he was going to be sick. He closed his eyes as the room began to spin. When he opened them again, the shine-eye entity was gone as if it had never been there in the first place.

Bender attempted to rationalize the incident. Perhaps in the five to ten seconds his eyes were closed the black-clad figure had gone to get some popcorn. Perhaps it was a kind of optical illusion. Such thoughts swirled through Bender's mind as he attempted to return his focus to the film, but his nerves were irrevocably on edge. And soon he once again felt that he was somehow being spied upon. The feeling became so strong a few minutes later that he was compelled to turn and look around.

To his horror, he saw right behind him the same man in black—who was indeed looking in his direction. The man had an impossibly unpleasant demeanor as he stared at Bender with unbridled anger and contempt. Now thoroughly spooked and unable to take any more, Bender got up and left the theater to head back to the safety of his stepfather's house. However, similarly strange MIB activity would plague Bender for the next few months without any real explanation—that is, until the MIB decided to formally introduce themselves to the panic-stricken UFO enthusiast.

Contact Day

Albert Bender was unnerved by the odd activity that seemed to surround him, but not too unnerved to invite even more of it upon himself! It seemed like a longshot even to him, but he was determined to force the issue of UFO contact by engaging in a "Contact Day" with his acolytes. It sounds a bit New Age, but Bender believed that the bridge across the great divide between Earthlings and extraterrestrials just might be a collective effort at telepathy!

It may sound like some sort of whimsical wishful thinking, but he truly believed that if he and his followers set aside a specific hour in which all of them would chant mental mantras demanding that ET give them a call, the UFO occupants—which Bender believed employed telepathic communication—would indeed respond. To be sure, two of his own board members adamantly rejected the proposal as nonsense, but they were overruled and the experiment went forward as planned.

Bender publicized his scheme in *The Space Review* and other official publications of the IFSB. He hoped that millions of people from the United States, Canada, and Europe would join in. Anyone who read the group's periodicals was requested to take part and given specific instructions on how to participate.

Called a "special bulletin", the missive read, "On March 15, all officers, representatives and members are asked to participate in an experiment—something that has not yet been attempted by any other group such as ours. We will attempt to send a message to the occupants of the saucers by the use of mental telepathy. Each member will memorize the message, and on the time designated will close his eyes in a quiet secluded spot, lie down if possible, and repeat this message in his mind."

Bender's mental message to ET was as follows:

Calling occupants of interplanetary craft! Calling occupants of interplanetary craft that have been observing our planet Earth. We of IFSB wish to make contact with you. We are your friends, and would like you to make an appearance here on Earth. Your presence before us will be welcomed with the utmost friendship. We will do all in our power to promote mutual understanding between your people and the people of Earth. Please come in peace and help us in our Earthly problems. Give us some sign that you have received our message. Be responsible for creating a miracle here on our planet to wake up the ignorant ones to reality. Let us hear from you. We are your friends.

If those words sound familiar to you, no, you aren't losing your mind. Because as an interesting aside to all this, about a decade or so later, the message Bender crafted for contacting UFOs was turned into a pop song, which was ultimately covered by the 70s music group The Carpenters. It remains to be seen if Karen Carpenter's hit song got any ET traction, but Albert Bender's original message most certainly did! Bender himself dutifully followed his own directions for Contact Day, and at exactly 6PM he dimmed the lighting of his attic, lay down flat on his back, and began repeating the predetermined message in his mind.

For Bender the third time really was the charm, because as soon as he repeated the words three times, he felt the temperature of the room drop and chills raced up his spine. He then developed a terrible headache, as if someone was slamming a sledgehammer down on top of his head. This was followed by the sulfurous smell of rotten eggs. If this was the kind of response ET was giving, it didn't appear to be as friendly a creature as Bender had hoped!

Bender relates that shortly after these unpleasant manifestations, he passed out with the odd feeling that his entire surroundings were fading out of existence. The next thing he knew, there were intense blue lights flashing all around him. His migraine headache grew worse, seemingly focused right above his eyes. Then, suddenly, the pain was gone, and to Bender's astonishment, he found himself floating directly above his own body! According to Bender's testimony, he was having an "out-of-body experience".

As he stared in disbelief at his own slumbering form below, he began to hear a distinct voice. The authoritative voice told him, "We have been watching you and your activities. Please be advised to discontinue delving into the mysteries of the universe. We will make an appearance if you disobey." Was this the response that he was looking for? A harsh rebuke for attempting contact in the first place? And rather than contact being a reward, the entity behind the words seemed to consider it a threat, telling him, "We will make an appearance if you disobey!"

This did not seem to be the friendly ET that Bender had longed to reach out to. Confused, he sent back the mental response, "Why aren't you friendly to us, as we do not mean to do any harm to you?" The cold voice bluntly replied, "We have a special assignment, and we must not be disturbed by your people." These beings were ready to admit their existence and their active mission on Earth, but did not want someone like Bender to interfere with their assignment. Whatever double-blind study the aliens were subjecting humanity to, they didn't want interlopers like Albert Bender to mess up their results.

The entity left with a parting remark for Bender, telling him in no uncertain terms, "We are among you and know your every move, so please be advised we are here on your Earth." Then, like a spell had just been broken, Bender opened his eyes and found himself back in his body—and for a split second, he could have sworn that a shadowy figure, dressed all in black, was standing nearby. But a split second later this apparition was gone as well, leaving Bender all alone in his anguish and confusion. Could it have all been just a bad dream?

It is certainly possible, but the event left a mark on Bender that he could not shake. Unlike other nightmares in which you're immensely relieved when you wake up from imminent danger, Bender's experience became a living, waking nightmare that would not leave him alone. Over the next few days he found himself so nauseated that he couldn't eat and grew physically ill. He also had immense trouble sleeping and was plagued with a general, severe lethargy that defied explanation. It was as if something—like some cosmic vampire—was sucking the life force right out of him.

Bender also found himself in quite a conundrum. He had experienced something truly unusual, but he didn't quite know how to explain it to others. He felt that no one would believe him and that he would become more of a laughingstock than he already was in many circles. He decided to stay quiet for the moment, write everything down in an unmarked letter, and lock it away inside the combination safe where he kept his valuables until he figured out what to do.

One possibility was to publish the account in *The Space Review*; another was to mail the letter to U.S. government officials to warn them about what he'd learned. Ultimately, he decided on publication. But when he unlocked his safe, the painstakingly crafted missive was nowhere to be seen—and that same strange smell of sulfur seemed to be pouring out of the now-empty safe. What was going on?

Albert Bender would receive his answer just a couple of weeks later when he had the same odd "dream"—if dream it was—that had plagued him on Contact Day. As soon as he drifted off to sleep, he found himself torn from his body and surrounded by flashing blue lights. This time, though, he could look around the room and discern that he was not alone. He could see three figures emerge from the darkness of the attic, dressed all in black. They looked like clergymen, except that they were all sporting fedoras on their heads. Although he couldn't tell which member of this MIB trio the voice came from, Bender could clearly hear the following words resonating in his head:

"You have dedicated yourself to the solution of the strange problem of unidentified objects in your atmosphere. Your interest is deep and sincere and you have devoted many hours to it. We also know that such interest and determination might lead to something that could bring you harm. We feel that you are a very good contact for us on your planet of Earth. You are an average person, and we know that what we tell you and show you will not be believed by anyone you might tell."

It is worth noting that this theme is often repeated in MIB stories: The entities inform their subjects that even if they did speak of what they witnessed, no one would believe them anyway.

Bender's visitors continued: "You are not a person of great renown on your planet; therefore, we have nothing to fear at present. We have a purpose for being here, and we will be here for some time yet. We must not be disturbed in our ultimate goal. As you see us here, we are not in our natural form. We have found it necessary to take on the look of your people while we are here."

After admitting that they could change shape at will, the MIB went on to explain, "This is mainly used as a means of returning here without being detected by anyone. We have made numerous contacts with Earth by means of craft from our own base, and at present we have craft hidden at a remote spot on your planet. We have found it necessary to go to great extremes at times to frighten off your Earth people and it has resulted in their deaths. We have also found it necessary to carry off Earth people to use their bodies to disguise our own."

After this startling admission, the MIB continued, "We wish to keep in touch with you and tell you many things because one day you will write about this, and we are certain that nobody will believe you, but you will be much wiser than anyone else on your planet. You will know what is out there in space, and you will know what the future holds for your mankind. You will see all three of us again, but we shall not reveal our names as they would mean nothing to you. Refer to us as Numbers 1, 2, and 3. We will answer according to number."

After these peculiar instructions, the beings left a parting gift, telling the terrified Bender, "We will leave you with a small piece of metal similar to your coins. It is to be kept in a secret place of your own. We wish to have you come with us at a time to be announced to you soon."

Bender then woke up to find himself clutching a strange, cold piece of metal in his hand. As he stared at the artifact, it seemed that what could otherwise be written off as a particularly vivid dream had crossed into irrefutable reality.

Bender Tenders his Resignation

Albert K. Bender's Sketch of a Man in Black

To his associates at the IFSB, Albert Bender seemed to be on the verge of something big. He alluded to recent developments that had him poised to crack the mystery of UFOs. But just as Bender was offering this tantalizing possibility of proof, he suddenly became completely silent on the subject.

Writer and veteran journalist Gray Barker, who was a close associate of Bender's and the Chief Investigator for the IFSB, experienced the abrupt change in Bender's demeanor firsthand, in 1953. Seemingly overnight, Bender went from being a zealous UFO evangelist to wanting nothing at all to do with UFOs. All Bender would tell his followers was that he had been visited by three men of authority who convinced him it would be best to shut down the IFSB. Without supplying any other reason, Bender then tendered his resignation as head of the IFSB.

Barker was so disturbed by Bender's sudden reversal that he took what he knew about the odd final days of the IFSB and wrote a book entitled *They Knew Too Much About Flying Saucers*. It was Barker who first posited the theory that there was some sort of secret organization actively attempting to silence any serious investigation of UFOs. According to Barker, as soon as anyone got close to unraveling the UFO enigma, they were visited by these strange men in black and mysteriously silenced. As Barker continued his analysis of what had befallen Bender, he came to the conclusion that the U.S. government knew much more about the UFO phenomenon than they were letting on. He even considered the possibility that the government might have cut some kind of secret deal with ET!

This veteran journalist placed the onus for such collaboration squarely on the shoulders of President Dwight D. Eisenhower. This was the mid-1950s, and Eisenhower was still in the midst of his first term. This timeline is of interest for conspiracy theorists, since one of the most popular alien conspiracy theories suggests that Eisenhower did in fact sign an official treaty with an extraterrestrial civilization during this exact period of time. But before this conspiracy theory was even a twinkling in some UFO's buff's eye, Gray Barker was openly speculating much the same thing: "Somehow, I have the feeling that President Eisenhower knows the utter futility of trying to preserve the peace of the world by stockpiling lethal weapons; I notice something of this in his recent speeches. Does old Army man Ike have definite knowledge of why saucers are here?"

Maybe—and to be clear, that is a big "maybe"—such an agreement between Ike and the aliens did take place, because Barker's speculations soon merited his very own encounter with an MIB. According to Barker, one of these dark entities appeared at the door of his office flashing one of his own newly minted business cards and demanding to know "what the card was all about". The card identified Barker as Chief Investigator for the now defunct IFSB. After Barker's terse explanation, the figure explained that the card had been found on a man who had been admitted to a local hospital. The victim had no proper identification on him, only the business card, so he was checking up on it as a potential lead. After Barker explained that he didn't know the man, the figure seemed to accept the answer and abruptly left his office.

It only dawned on Barker after the MIB's departure that it would have been virtually impossible for an unknown man laid up in a hospital to have one of his business cards: They had been printed just days before! The whole encounter now seemed far too odd for him to swallow the explanation that the mystery visitor had given him.

Even though the U.S. branch of the IFSB was officially out of commission now, the British and Australian branches had chosen to go on, and it would be the director of the Australian branch, a dogged UFO investigator named Edgar Jarrold, who would become the next target of the MIB. Soon after Bender's resignation, Jarrold began to see a black Cadillac routinely parked outside of his office. This wasn't all that unusual in itself, but he had never noticed it before, and now it was being parked right outside on a daily basis. Who was the owner of this shiny black car and what was his business? Jarrold was about to find out, because soon enough he was seeing not only the car but a pair of strange looking men dressed in black sitting inside it.

It seemed that every time he peered out his window, these strange figures were staring right back at him. There was no apparent reason for this stare-down, but there they were, seated in their dark-colored vehicle staring away. Following these menacing occurrences, Jarrold began to receive mysterious phone calls which he intuitively knew were connected to the mysterious men loitering outside his office. Shortly thereafter, Jarrold began to face harassment of an even more unconventional kind in the form of poltergeist activity.

He heard strange, unexplained knocking sounds in and around his home, and household items began disappearing and appearing in different places. Jarrold had entered into a realm that UFO researcher and paranormal connoisseur John Keel would term "high strangeness". This strangeness continued over the next few weeks until it escalated into physical violence when Jarrold was pushed down a flight of stairs by an unseen force. This occurred right in the middle of the afternoon at a popular department store in the Australian capital of Sydney.

This was the last straw for Jarrold. Just like Bender before him, he was forced to acknowledge the success of the paranormal bullying campaign and turn in his resignation from the Australian branch of the IFSB. Jarrold and Bender had frequently held detailed conference calls, and it has been suggested that Bender let Jarrold in on more of his secret findings than anyone else. If this is the case, it would seem that after the MIB silenced Bender, they went to the next link in the chain of knowledge and began an ultimately successful campaign to put him out of business as well.

Gray Barker, who at first was supportive of Bender's account, ultimately became skeptical about the MIB's supposedly paranormal nature. Barker was convinced that the Men in Black were simply government agents. However, Edgar Jarrold's experience, which occurred several thousand miles away in Australia, along with subsequent similar accounts of others, seems to support the idea that the Men in Black may be part of something much further reaching than any agency on Earth.

The MIB Charade Continues

Just who are the MIB? Aliens masquerading as humans? Humans masquerading as aliens? For those who encounter these odd figures, such oddly juxtaposed questions seem frustratingly appropriate. Just take the case of Cynthia Appleton, an unassuming British housewife with no prior interest in the paranormal, who was suddenly beset by one of the most bewildering of phenomena. Her harrowing tale began on the afternoon of November 16th, 1957, when after walking into her living room she was suddenly overcome with a feeling of immense oppression, as if she were being bombarded by a tremendous force.

Cynthia watched as an intense illumination filled her entire home, and then apparently had an episode of what UFO researchers have long referred to as "missing time". She looked at the clock and saw that it was an hour later, but she had no recollection of what had occurred in that hour—and no rational explanation as to what had happened. Had she simply been daydreaming for an hour straight? As unlikely as that explanation seemed, it was initially the only one she had to go on.

But this wasn't the only strange happening to beset Cynthia Appleton, and soon no amount of rationalization would suffice. Two days later, on November 18th, she experienced a sequel to the 16th's opening salvos of the paranormal. Just past three in the afternoon, Cynthia ventured to her upstairs nursery to check on her sleeping child. When she happened to look out the window, she was struck by just how "rosy pink" the sky had become. As she admired the unique cast the sky had taken on, she suddenly felt the same intense pressure she had felt two days before.

Just like before, she felt a strange energy coursing through her, giving her goose bumps and causing her hair to stand on end. Cynthia then heard a strange, high-pitched humming sound emanating seemingly from nowhere and everywhere all at once. The sound rapidly grew louder, and soon the hum felt like it was vibrating through her entire body. The vibration increased in intensity until Cynthia felt that her very molecular structure was about to be ripped asunder, but then, just as mysteriously as the phenomenon had begun, it stopped.

As she regained her composure, she was alarmed to see a strange haze appear before her. This haze swirled and convoluted itself until it began to pixelate like an image from a staticky old TV. Then, as if someone had finally found the sweet spot on the tuning dial, the haze snapped into crystal clarity and the holographic projection of a strangely dressed man appeared.

The creature was mostly human-looking at six feet in height, with delicate facial structure, extremely light skin, blond hair, and blue eyes. He was wearing a spacesuit, something akin to that worn by NASA's Apollo astronauts, even though the encounter predated the Apollo program by several years.

At first, Cynthia was understandably terrified at the sight, but the strange being quickly told her not to be afraid. In fact, the voice repeated the instruction over and over in her head, until somehow she simply wasn't afraid!

It seemed that the being had the ability to calm her down at will, and some have since pointed out similarities between Cynthia's encounter and several accounts of angelic visitation in the Bible. After all, every single time an angel appears in the Bible, the first words it utters are always "Be not afraid." Before the angel could impart its message, it always took the time to calm the rattled nerves of the recipient. The illuminated figure before Cynthia certainly seemed to be operating under a similar protocol, but if this was an angel, it soon deviated from the traditional narrative.

The being informed Cynthia that he came from a planet called Gharnasvarn. This spaceman then motioned with his hands to draw a holographic screen out of thin air. This screen showed Cynthia images of the being's planet and associated spacecraft.

So far, of course, Cynthia's encounters did not much resemble MIB incidents. Shortly after these introductory experiences, however, the same character reappeared accompanied by two others—not as a holographic projection, and not aboard a UFO, but in a black MIB-style Cadillac!

The car rolled right up to Cynthia's home, the entities knocked on her door, and Cynthia answered it to find them standing on her doorstep garbed in complete Men in Black attire. Having ditched his spacesuit for a fedora, her friendly Nordic-looking visitor was now decked out as an MIB! From February to August 1958, all subsequent visits by the beings took on a decidedly MIB cast, with the entities—whatever they were—knocking on her door, as any real, physical human being would do. But despite their human clothing and human car, these "men" were clearly not normal.

During the course of one visit, one of the MIB mentioned that he had accidentally hurt himself prior to his arrival. He then showed Cynthia a finger that appeared to be badly burned. But before Cynthia could rush off to grab a standard first aid kit to treat her guest, the MIB directed her to simply bring him a bowl of hot water. The Man in Black dipped his finger into the bowl before pulling out a toothpaste-like tube and squeezing some kind of gel onto his burned skin. According to Cynthia Appleton, as soon as the substance touched the burn, his injury was instantaneously healed.

The MIB then simply walked out the door. Cynthia followed him outside and watched as he hopped into the black Cadillac and took off down the street. But the MIB had left a present behind: Floating in the water bowl the being had used to cool his finger, Cynthia found a piece of his dead skin which had apparently flaked off during the healing process. After Cynthia came forward with her story, this artifact was sent off to a laboratory where it was examined with best electron microscopes of the day.

It was determined that the skin was not human, but it could hardly be deemed alien either. It seemed to be closely related to animal tissue, such as that of a pig. Several decades later, when scientists realized the magnitude of the similarities between pig and human DNA, some would speculate that the skin this MIB left behind may have been of this consistency because it was not naturally occurring but had been grown in a lab. The skin sample contained proteins similar to those used to grow tissue in Petri dishes.

The conclusion behind such speculation is that the MIB are not naturally born beings but some kind of clones that were grown in a lab somewhere. But then again, perhaps Cynthia made the whole story up, and the reason why the bit of skin found in her water bowl resembles pig tissue is because she dropped a piece of pork inside of it! At any rate, true or false, besides the later appearance of black cars, black clothes, and odd behavior, her account of these MIB differs considerably from the standard narrative.

In most accounts, MIB appear only after a separate UFO event has occurred, and their main objective is to convince the witness to not speak out or come forward with what they have seen. On the contrary, these MIB seemed to appear simply for the sake of appearing. There was no previous sighting that might have gotten their attention. And instead of insisting that Cynthia "forget about UFOs" as most other MIB seem to do, these MIB actually encouraged discourse about them and even showed Cynthia holographic images of spacecraft!

Such strange incidents only make the motivation behind the Men in Black all the murkier. Just what are these strange Men in Black up to? Do they have an objective to fulfill, or are they just out to pull a fast one upon humanity? Whoever these cosmic tricksters may be, for the time being, they appear to be completely content to allow their odd little charade to continue.

The Solway Firth Spaceman

The Solway Firth is a body of water that runs between Scotland and England, and its main significance is the role it plays in demarcating the border between the two countries. But on May 24, 1964, the banks of the firth would become the backdrop of a decidedly unusual event.

It all began when a local man named Jim Templeton took his wife and kids on a Sunday outing to the nearby Burgh Marsh to relax in the outdoors and take some family photos. The Templetons didn't meet anyone else on their way, and they believed that they were all alone on the firth. It seemed like a perfect time for Jim to test out his camera and snap some shots without any interference. There shouldn't have been anyone there to ruin the pictures by stepping into the frame, but he was in for a surprise when he had his photos developed a week later. Before he even looked at them, the clerk who handed him the prints made the odd remark, "Jim, you have some nice photographs, but it is a pity that the best one has been spoiled by that man in the background wearing a spacesuit."

Jim initially shrugged off the remark as some sort of offbeat attempt at humor. But when the clerk made another mention of the odd cameo in the photograph, he pulled out the pictures to take a look for himself. He was shocked to see exactly what the young woman had been referring to. In what should have been a normal photo of his daughter during their Sunday picnic at Solway Firth, there was a mysterious figure, clad in what could indeed be described only as some sort of spacesuit, standing directly behind her, staring right at the camera.

This being had been invisible to Jim when he took the picture, yet showed up clear as day in the developed photograph. Jim was as much perplexed as he was alarmed by the photo, and not knowing what else to do, he went down to the police station to see if they could help clear the matter up for him. When the photo reached the desk of Police Superintendent Donald Roy of the Carlisle Police Department, he didn't know what to make of it. He could clearly see the odd figure, and since this was many decades before Photoshop and other means of digitally altering photographs, there could be no question that the strange character had actually been at Solway Firth. But what was it?

Superintendent Roy had no idea. Frustrated as he was, he readily admitted defeat, telling Jim, "I don't know the answer to this one." The photo was then shipped off to a special investigation lab to be inspected further. The lab absolutely ruled out any possibility of double exposure or superimposed imaging in the photograph. Whatever appeared in the image was indeed there when the picture was taken.

When the strange story became public, theories from UFO enthusiasts began to pour in. Many theorized that the entity in the photo must have somehow been invisible to human sight, perhaps because it was popping in and out of dimensional space at such a high rate of speed that it was only detectable by the split-second shutter of Jim's camera. It was a longshot theory, but it was about as good as any other explanation on offer.

In the middle of this rampant speculation, the MIB made their presence known. A little later that summer, Jim's wife answered the phone to find a man at the other end apparently eager to investigate the photo. Jim wanted to get to the bottom of the picture just as much as anyone else, so he didn't hesitate. He readily agreed to have this so-called investigator visit his home. Two days later, a black car pulled up in the Templetons' driveway and two men dressed all in black came to their door. At first the men were fairly polite, but the conversation took a menacing turn when they began probing deeper into the circumstances in which Jim had taken the photo. Soon the men were outright demanding that Jim get in their car and lead them to the exact spot.

Jim understandably had his reservations, but it was as if he couldn't refuse. He meekly agreed to take them and piled into the MIB black car. As soon as they arrived at Solway Firth, the questioning became an outright interrogation, with the MIB forcing Jim to recount every last detail of his last time there. The mysterious men insisted on hearing seemingly trivial bits of information such as the exact weather conditions and the kinds of wildlife present at the time the photo was taken. They seemed to be specifically interested in the mannerisms of any cows or sheep that had been on the scene. Jim was dumbfounded at the odd questions that seemed to have so little to do with the photo in question, but he felt forced to answer them regardless.

The men then changed tactics. Seeming determined to catch Jim in a lie, they began to repeatedly ask him who the person in the photo really was.

One demanded, "Show me where the man was of whom you took the picture!"

Jim stuttered, "Wh–what man?"

For the next several minutes, they repeatedly insinuated that Jim had collaborated with someone else to hoax the photo. Jim was adamant, however, and steadfastly insisted that there was no one else at Solway Firth when he took the photo that day. Finally, the MIB simply glanced at each other and shrugged. Then one of them responded quietly, "Oh—right," and the two abruptly turned and walked back toward their car.

Jim was so stunned by this abrupt departure that he simply stood and stared as they got back into the car. Suddenly realizing that he was about to be stranded several miles from home, he tried to chase after them, but he was too late. Not waiting for Jim, the MIB drove away at a high rate of speed. Jim had to walk home alone—but compared with others who have faced far worse from the Men in Black, he should probably count himself lucky for the walk.

Unmasking the Imposters

It was a clear day on August 3, 1965, and Rex Heflin was running the road as an Orange County, California, highway inspector. His chief concern was an overgrown tree that was blocking a railroad crossing sign. Fearing that drivers wouldn't slow down for the crossing in time, Heflin made it his number-one priority to get the offending tree removed. He turned on his radio to ask headquarters to send a tree trimming crew, but when he did so he found that the airwaves were completely silent.

Hoping that it was just a temporary malfunction, he was trying to contact HQ again when he noticed something moving in his peripheral vision. When he looked up at the sky ahead of him, he saw an "unidentified object" moving across the horizon. It was startlingly close to his position on the ground, but it made no sound. Heflin watched in utter amazement as this floating skyscraper, which he estimated to be about 150 feet in length, sailed serenely through the air. Reaching for his government-issue camera, Heflin quickly snapped a photograph of the anomalous object.

He was able to take two more photos of the craft before it left his field of vision. These photos are perhaps some of the best close-ups of a UFO ever made, showing a detailed depiction of complex machinery on the craft's underbelly and a searchlight shining down onto the road. All of these things would have been very hard to hoax in 1965. However, Heflin himself was not all that impressed with his photos. He firmly believed that he had not seen any ET spaceship but merely some sort of hitherto unknown top-secret aircraft flown by the U.S. military.

When he showed the photos to his friends, however, they did not share his opinion. One of them was so astounded by the captivating images that he eventually persuaded the reluctant Heflin to take the photos to the local paper. Once the pictures were circulating in the media, Heflin's life began to change. First, UFO groups began to excitedly descend upon him to hear his story. Then, shortly after shooing the UFO enthusiasts away, Heflin had to contend with officials from area military bases who wished to examine the pictures, probably to ascertain whether the craft was theirs.

Seeing that it was not, the local brass handed the images back to Heflin. But this wouldn't be his only interaction with a supposed military authority, because shortly after the pictures were returned to him he received a visit from someone claiming to be from the North American Air Defense Command (NORAD). The man was dressed in a typical MIB dark suit and flashed some sort of quasi-official looking badge for identification. This supposed government representative claimed that he also needed to borrow the photos for further study.

Since the pictures had been readily returned after he loaned them to other military installations, Heflin didn't hesitate to hand them over to the mysterious stranger. But after several weeks passed without word as to when he would get his photos back, he contacted NORAD to ask. However, the agency denied that any of their representatives had visited him. As the Chief of Staff explained, "For your information, NORAD does not have the responsibility for evaluation of UFOs and therefore would not knowingly be in the business of collecting UFO pictures for evaluation."

Heflin realized that the man who confiscated his photos had been an imposter—but an imposter from where? And for what purpose? This was something that many branches of the US military and intelligence services were apparently trying to figure out as well. Since then, through the Freedom of Information Act, several official memos and documents have come to light indicating that the U.S. government was just as puzzled about the MIB as anyone else and was actively seeking to unmask the imposter.

An official document from the U.S. Air Force dated March 1, 1967, is entitled "Impersonation of Air Force Officers". This is a clear indication that although the Air Force did not know who the MIB was, they were gravely concerned that he was attempting to present himself as a NORAD agent. The memo, written by Lieutenant General Hewitt Wheless, gave a brief description of Heflin's encounter with the imposter and also described a subsequent case of MIB interference in which a man dressed in dark Air Force fatigues intimidated citizens and even police officers who had witnessed a UFO. In that case, the imposter briskly informed them that "they did not see what they thought they saw and that they should not talk to anyone about the sighting".

The top brass apparently had no idea as to the identity of these imposters who were so brazenly threatening U.S. citizens and telling them what "they had seen" and "not seen". After relaying these eyewitness accounts of the MIB, the memo ended by imploring any Air Force personnel who encountered such activity, or heard others mention it, to send all details about the episode directly to the Office of Special Investigations (OSI), a specialized Air Force intelligence branch.

That same year, the University of Colorado began the infamous Condon Report on UFOs. Led by Dr. Edward Condon, it sought to investigate the best UFO info that could be gleaned from the U.S. Air Force's own official investigation of unidentified flying objects—Project Blue Book. Heflin's UFO sighting and subsequent encounter with the MIB would be one of the many subjects of the Condon Report. In fact, the Report Coordinator, Robert Low, who conducted an interview with Heflin, rated his case as being among the top four of the entire report.

Apparently the MIB were taking notice as well, because it was right in the middle of Dr. Condon's investigation that Heflin received his second visit from the mysterious Men in Black. This time they pulled up at his home inside a pitch-black vehicle that seemed to have a strange glow emanating from it. Through dark tinted windows, Heflin could see the outline of someone seated in the car. Then two men dressed in Air Force uniforms got out—apparently more MIB imposters ready for more mischief. These MIB accosted Heflin and immediately began hounding him with an endless barrage of questions on all of the recent UFO sightings in the area. Oddly, they also brought up people who had disappeared in and around the distant UFO hotspot of the Bermuda Triangle.

As soon as the two men entered his house, Heflin could feel a strange static charge in the air. His radio, which had been left on, began to emit wild popping sounds. Although the men did not exactly come right out and threaten him, Heflin recalls that their whole demeanor seemed threatening. For the most part, they simply talked to him about recent UFO sightings that had little if anything to do with him, but they seemed incredibly aggressive and agitated as they did so. Just picture two grown men in Air Force fatigues standing in your living room going on and on about UFOs, voices raised, wildly gesticulating with their hands, and you get the idea.

As they rambled on and on, Heflin could barely get a word in. He felt as if he were literally a captive audience to the long-winded, agitated diatribe. But Heflin had learned a thing or two since his first MIB encounter, and this time (when he managed to break through the incessant chatter) he insisted on knowing the full names and ranks of the two men who were ranting and raving in his living room. Surprisingly, the MIB obliged this request—but when Heflin later checked with the USAF, it found no-one in its records matching the names and ranks that the two men had given.

John Keel Enters into the Mystery

Writer and investigative journalist into all things paranormal John Keel was the first person to use the exact term "Men in Black". Keel's association with the MIB began after a December 15, 1966, incident in which a group of West Virginia teenagers encountered something they could not explain. The teens were haunting a local hangout called the "TNT Area". This place was home to vast stockpiles of explosives that had been stored there ever since the outbreak of World War Two.

Parked in this secluded spot, they were playfully laughing and cavorting around with each other in their car. In the midst of this revelry, they suddenly spotted something very unusual in the rearview mirror. Standing directly to the rear of the car was a bizarre entity standing some seven feet in height. It had moth-like wings wrapped around its body and eyes that shone through the darkness like fire. The driver hit the gas instantly and the terrified teens sped off to the police station to report what they had seen.

Deputy Millard Halstead took down the details of their account. As bizarre as their tale was, and as reluctant as Halstead was to enter such oddities into the official police record, he knew these kids well. And these kids were just not the sort to make up wild stories for no reason. Besides which, if they were acting, they deserved an academy award, because Halstead was convinced from speaking with them that they were frightened out of their minds.

This was not a fanciful fit of youthful attention seeking; these kids had clearly been subjected to sheer terror. But by what? Deputy Halstead put on a brave face and volunteered to escort them back to the scene of the sighting for another look. But the search turned up nothing. Whatever had spooked this group of friends was long gone.

Despite Halstead's inability to track the monster, by the following morning it was clear that this entity had been busy. Similar reports were popping up all over the area, and the inventive locals had already developed a name for the beast: they called it the Mothman.

The strange happenings in West Virginia are the stuff of legend, and it was in reporting these frightening tales that John Keel became famous. The stories reek of "high strangeness", and their telling has been buried in layer upon layer of complexity. For the purpose of this book, it's not necessary to go into all the details—but just know that it was while Keel was investigating the Mothman that he came face to face with the MIB.

Before Keel encountered the MIB, though, he was receiving reports of a WIB—a Woman in Black! Apparently, soon after sightings of the Mothman, an unknown woman would appear at the doors of witnesses carrying a clipboard. After falsely introducing herself as an associate or secretary of Keel's, this woman peppered the witnesses with all manner of questions on UFOs and other paranormal happenings in classic MIB style. And just like the MIB, she often had an uncanny knowledge and insight into the personal lives of those she pestered, making them especially uneasy by revealing private details of their health and lifestyle.

Several people wrote to Keel to complain, asking him not to send his "secretary" around to bother them anymore. Keel, of course, was bewildered and promptly informed them that he had no such hired help! Whoever this woman was, she was not working for John Keel. The encounters with this WIB were accompanied by the classic dark Cadillacs associated with the Men in Black, which were seen roaming the streets at all hours of the day.

These cars would park on the side of the road or pull into driveways, and then men claiming to be various kinds of federal employees, social workers or census takers, would get out and canvas the neighborhood. Similar to the WIB before them, these MIB would ask sensitive questions about their targets health. Even odder, on other occasions the MIB didn't attempt to interview Mothman witnesses at all. They simply arrived with some kind of petty request. One popular tactic with these MIB was to frantically pound on someone's door just to ask for a cup of water!

These stories are so bizarre you could hardly make them up, and as the high strangeness of these MIB continued apace with the ongoing Mothman sightings, the citizens of West Virginia felt that they were being besieged. Their suspicion seemed confirmed when innocent questions about water turned into an all-out assault as the MIB began to take a much more hostile approach.

High schooler Connie Carpenter was one of those who fell victim to this frightening MIB aggression when on February 22, 1967, one of the MIB apparently attempted to kidnap her. According to Connie, one of the strange dark cars that had been plaguing the area pulled up to her and a man dressed all in black got out and asked her for directions. But as Connie prepared to answer, the man suddenly lunged at her and tried to drag her into the vehicle with him. Fortunately, she was able to break away and make a run for it. But late that evening, as she was attempting to assuage her shattered nerves in the comfort of her home, a note mysteriously appeared under her door with the menacing message "Be careful, girl. I can get you yet."

We have to keep in mind that it is entirely possible that this incident had nothing to do with the ongoing MIB activity. The man in question may not have been a Man in Black; he could have been just your average opportunistic kidnapper. Nevertheless, the whole community was at its breaking point because of the barrage of negative activity.

As the principal investigator of the phenomenon, John Keel naturally gained the attention of the MIB as well. In fact, even after he left West Virginia, the activity would follow him back to New York!

Keel often mentioned Men in Black types apparently following or monitoring him as he walked through the streets of Manhattan. On one occasion he even received a strange phone call asking him to come to Long Island to discuss his work. When he did, the MIB told him in no uncertain terms to end his inquest into the Mothman sightings—or "something bad would happen" to him.

Meanwhile, back in Point Pleasant, West Virginia, citizens were facing still more threatening situations at the hands of the visiting Men in Black. One young woman we'll call Jane Doe had a particularly harrowing experience when immediately after a UFO sighting, she encountered a WIB similar to the one described earlier. This entity brusquely informed that she had been chosen for further "contact". Contact with whom? Soon after this, a black Cadillac pulled up beside her and a man attired as a classic MIB approached her, introduced himself as "Apol", and then quickly retreated back into his car, leaving the bewildered young woman standing by herself on the street corner attempting to sort out just what had transpired.

A few days after this odd introduction, Apol showed up at her house. In bizarrely routine fashion, after knocking on her door, this MIB asked for a cup of water, which he said he needed to "take some pills". After taking his pills, Apol handed three of the pills over to Jane and directed her to swallow one of them. As leery as anyone would be of such a request by a random stranger at the door, Jane felt compelled to obey. As soon as she took the pill, she felt dizzy and was overwhelmed by a horrible migraine pounding through her forehead.

Keel later had one of the remaining pills examined and determined that it was composed of some sort of sulfur compound. Interestingly enough, at the time of these sightings, while the clandestine MK Ultra mind control program was in full gear, the CIA was actively experimenting with the supposed truth serum, sodium thiopental. This drug is a sulfur compound as well; in fact, the FDA lists it as a "sulfur analogue of sodium pentobarbital". Was the MIB who accosted Jane attempting to load his unwitting victim up with some similar serum in order to get the truth out of her?

Shortly after this episode, a more alarming case occurred in which a woman named Jaye Paro actually *was* kidnapped by an MIB in a black Cadillac. As Jaye struggled in the passenger seat of the car, she noticed that the dashboard of the vehicle was lit up with flashing lights that seemed to have an almost hypnotic effect on her. Strangely, the car interior smelled like a hospital, and the odor became even worse when her captors held a small vial of a sulfurous substance under her nose while asking her all manner of questions. Was it another dose of truth serum? At any rate, after this interrogation session was over, the MIB simply dropped Jaye off where they had picked her up.

Soon after this incident, Keel interviewed the first recipient of undue MIB attention, Jane Doe, who had been accosted by the entity who called himself Apol. This being had apparently been instructing Jane Doe about troubling events that were soon to occur in the Middle East, and even more alarmingly he had asked Jane to pass on to Keel the warning that something very bad was about to happen to Bobby Kennedy. This was still a few years before RFK's assassination, so the prediction is a bit uncanny in its accuracy. Understandably alarmed to receive such a message, Keel asked the young woman to come into his office so that he could hypnotically regress her for more information.

To his shock, once he put her under hypnosis, he found himself speaking not to Jane but to Apol himself. Incredibly, the MIB claimed to be parked nearby so he could manipulate Jane's vocal cords and use her as a living communication device. One explanation for all this would be that Jane was suffering from some sort of psychosis and Apol was just one of her own multiple personalities. On the other hand, more than a few of Apol's predictions did in indeed come to fruition. Robert Kennedy was slain by an assassin's bullet not long afterwards, and many of the other political upheavals predicted have occurred as well.

Why did this entity who went by Apol claim such intimate knowledge of future world events? This is where Keel's narrative of the MIB of West Virginia takes another strange twist. As Keel continued his discourse with Apol—who was actually calling Keel on the telephone now—the entity claimed that he was "trapped in time" and forced to "jump about from past to future".

If the story wasn't weird enough already, here was yet another fantastical layer to the MIB enigma. What were the MIB? Government agents performing PSYOPS? Aliens covering their tracks? Lost time travelers? Perhaps a combination of all three? Keel would later assert his belief that the MIB were a whole new level of entity from somewhere just beyond our perception—beings he termed "ultra-terrestrials".

John Keel had sought to unravel an incredible story when he launched his investigation into the strange happenings in West Virginia—but in many ways, he only deepened the mystery.

Further Misadventures with the MIB

After John Keel first gave the phenomenon its name in the late 1960s, the Men in Black continued their sporadic visits to those associated with UFOs. These encounters could be frightening, they could be intimidating, but just as often, they could be comically absurd. Just take the example of a woman whose name comes down to us as simply "Mrs. B". In October of 1967, Mrs. B was minding her own business at her home in Luis Valley, Colorado, when a man dressed in black showed up unannounced at her door. Mrs. B had recently seen a UFO, and the man seemed to know all about it.

He also seemed to know all about many other things as well, even though he was admittedly illiterate. This strange MIB took one look at Mrs. B's home library and stated, "I cannot read, but mention any book in any library and I will be able to tell you its contents." He then seemed to take offense at the fact that Mrs. B kept a well-stocked kitchen, complaining that humanity wastes "too much time and energy on food" and asserting that it would be better if human beings simply took their nourishment directly "out of the atmosphere".

The man then stumbled upon a painting Mrs. B had recently made of her UFO sighting and told her he wanted to buy it. Mrs. B took pride in her work, so she set high value on the item—whereupon the dismayed MIB informed her that he had no money. The entity then said his goodbyes, went out the door and hopped in his car to leave. Having been in a kind of strange trance throughout the visit, Mrs. B came to her senses as the car was pulling away and had enough presence of mind to jot down the car's license plate number. But when she took it to the police station the next day, they couldn't find a match.

On the surface these stories sound completely ridiculous. The number one question that comes to mind is, why would you let these weird characters into your home in the first place? In many MIB encounters, as strange as the MIB are, the people who encounter them feel some irresistible urge to entertain their odd guests. People who normally wouldn't open the door for anyone who came uninvited find themselves holding it wide open for the MIB. Not only that, they seem somehow forced to play along with the whole charade, no matter how ridiculous it is. They have some semblance of control, just as Mrs. B exhibited by insisting a high price be paid for her artwork, but in the presence of the MIB, normal judgment has been suspended. The MIB's host can thus be cajoled into participating in the absurd scenarios the MIB comes up with.

Many have pointed out the great similarity between this aspect of MIB lore and that of the far older tales of fairies. In almost all classic fairy stories, as soon as the fairies present themselves to someone, it is as if everything around them is suddenly enchanted. Nothing is quite normal, or like it should be—including the willpower to resist the strange games that the fairies have people play for them.

In UFO lore, this experience is sometimes referred to as the "Oz Factor" in reference to the Wizard-of-Oz-like moment when reality itself seems to be bending to the will of the UFOs and their occupants. Are the MIB just a modern variant of the ancient fairy phenomenon? Well, just like the fickle fairies of old, these modern-day tricksters can't seem to get their stories straight. At times they lie and claim to be from the CIA, FBI, Air Force, you name it—and then at other times they own up to being aliens, time travelers, or some other kind of (as the late John Keel has termed it) ultra-terrestrials.

In the case of a UFO investigator named Peggy, who was plagued by MIB in late 1967, one of the entities that accosted her stated that he and his brethren were indeed part of a vast conspiracy—a Cosmic Brotherhood, no less. The incident occurred at a department store in Schenectady, New York, where Peggy—because being a UFO investigator doesn't always pay the bills—was working part-time. One day a security guard made a beeline for her as if he had something important to say. Since the man was part of the security detail, Peggy naturally assumed that it must be security related, but she turned out to be completely mistaken.

What the man actually wanted to tell her was that he was a member of a secret organization called the Cosmic Brotherhood. Now, one might suspect that this man had somehow heard that Peggy was a UFO investigator on the side and was just messing around with her. But because of what happened next—at least according to Peggy's account—the possibility that this was an attempt at humor was immediately cast by the wayside.

Another coworker happened to overhear the guard make this strange proclamation and quipped, "This guy is nuts!"

This put-down led the guard to respond, "If you don't get away from here and forget what you heard, I will turn into the most horrible thing you've ever seen."

As the coworker was preparing a cutting comeback, rays of light began to emanate from the guard's eyes. Completely spooked, the man made himself scarce. Shortly after this encounter, he quit the job and was never heard from again.

Was this an MIB posing as a run-of-the-mill security guard? Many of the things he said match the typical mannerisms of the MIB. When accosted by the interloping coworker, the guard told him to forget what he had heard. This is standard MIB protocol: singling out one person (in this case Peggy) for communication but ordering others to forget everything they have witnessed. Besides silencing others, in many cases the MIB appear to be power-mad control freaks intent on letting their targets know that they are watching them and can interfere with their lives at any time they choose.

This was most certainly the case with one Reverend Martin. Rev. Martin was a fairly progressive pastor who even allowed his children to engage in Halloween festivities, and so on the Halloween night of 1968, he and his 4-year-old girl were trick-or-treating. While going door to door with his daughter to ask for candy, the Reverend happened to see a light move across the dimming horizon in his peripheral vision.

Turning to get a better look at the object, he could see the unusual shining light moving in strange patterns across the nighttime sky. He quietly watched as the object suddenly shot off at tremendous speed and left his frame of vision. The whole sequence of events lasted only a few seconds, but even after turning in for the night, Rev. Martin couldn't get the sighting out of his mind. And as he fell into slumber on that All Hollow's Eve, the Reverend had a terrible dream in which he was visited by a horrifying entity that instructed him not to talk about the UFO he had seen.

The following morning, Rev. Martin, ready to leave the ghouls and goblins of Halloween behind him, returned to his duties in the sanctuary and busied himself with his chores at the church. But he had a hard time focusing on what he was doing, and he just couldn't shake the feeling that he was being observed by some hidden, menacing figure. He felt that hidden eyes were carefully tracking each step he made.

As he called it a day and left the sanctuary to go home, the feeling became stronger. For a moment he thought he even heard the sound of someone walking behind him. Wanting to catch his stalker in the act, Rev. Martin spun around to see who was approaching—and to his shock he glimpsed a strange figure dressed in black ducking down behind a truck just as he turned. Who was this person playing hide and seek in the church parking lot? Was it just some kind of coincidence? Did the person just happen to stoop down to pick something up right when Rev. Martin turned? Or was this MIB shenanigans of the highest order?

The events of the next few days would prove it to be the latter. And as things progressed, Rev. Martin wasn't the only one to encounter MIB activity. His kids began reporting that strange men in black would appear and disappear in their bedrooms at night. From the outset, Rev. Martin's MIB encounters were much more overtly paranormal than the more "textbook" MIB manifestations. There were no black Cadillacs appearing in the driveway to signal an MIB interview; like Bender's MIB, these Men in Black just materialized at will.

The family endured this unusual activity for some time before Rev. Martin's wife decided to leave and take the kids with her. The Reverend had almost been expecting the separation, and he was glad to accept it if it would allow his family to escape the torment they were being subjected to. He was left to face his tormentors alone, and the high strangeness of MIB activity would continue to haunt him in various ways throughout the succeeding years.

Finally, on the tenth anniversary of the night he first saw the UFO, this strange MIB variant decided to introduce itself fully to the Reverend. On that Halloween night, while he was still wide awake, several entities materialized in front of him, all at once. The creatures were short, bald, and shaped like men, but had a decidedly inhuman cast. As Rev. Martin stared in shock, the apparent leader of the group stated that he just wanted to make sure that the Reverend didn't have any hard feelings toward them because of all the pranks they had pulled over the years.

The entities then informed him that they could change their appearance at will—and as if to prove it, they began to transform into all manner of fantastic creatures, morphing into angels one second, aliens the next, as well as Bigfoot, goblins, trolls, and all manner of other creatures of myth and legend that haunt the human consciousness. Surprisingly, they allowed Rev. Martin to take photos while they performed these fantastic feats. Thinking that he was finally going to have the evidence he needed to show the world that he wasn't crazy after all, he took several shots of their transformations. The MIB then departed, apparently with no reservations at all about the evidence they had left behind. This, of course, is a stark contrast to how MIB usually behave, since their goal is typically to confiscate supernatural evidence, not create it!

But the story doesn't end there. Before Rev. Martin could show anyone the photographs, he received yet another knock on his door and found two police officers standing on his doorstep. The pair told him not to worry, because they weren't there on official business; they had just heard that he had some interesting information on UFOs. This would have seemed quite odd under normal circumstances, but as is so often the case with MIB visits, the Oz Factor of suspended reality took hold, and Rev. Martin readily invited the "officers" inside. When he showed them his photos, they expressed their approval of the rare documentation, and congratulated him that this bit of evidence would be a great vindication for "his work" (presumably in the field of UFO research). Seemingly well satisfied, they left.

The same men returned just a few hours later, however, and this time their attitude had drastically transformed from feigned curiosity to outright aggression. As soon as Rev. Martin opened the door, without saying a word they shoved their way into his home, ransacked the place, and took his photos. The "police" then threw the clergyman into the back of their vehicle and took him for a ride. From the back of the squad car, he listened in horror as the men in front murmured about what to do with his body. But instead of killing him, they simply dropped him off in the middle of nowhere and left him to find his own way back home.

It was only then that Rev. Martin finally understood that the "police" who had knocked on his door were not really police. Just like the security guard who accosted the UFO investigator in Schenectady, New York, was not a security guard, and the NORAD Air Force officers who hounded Rex Heflin were not Air Force personnel, these cops were nothing more than—Men in Black!

Silent Witnesses to the MIB

Peter and Sandra Taylor were in the middle of a late-night drive home across the English countryside on August 16, 1972, when the radio began wildly oscillating from station to station. Shortly after the onset of this odd interference, the Taylors looked out the driver's side window to see a brightly lit craft attempting to land behind a group of trees. As they followed the winding road, they were startled to see that the object had landed in a spot that they would pass right by.

Peter, more than a bit unnerved, took the car down to a cautiously slow speed as they stared out at the kaleidoscope of colors that the strange vehicle was emitting. The craft was shaped like a large melon and had flashing lights crisscrossing all around its surface. As they continued to gaze at it, the Taylors noticed that there were other cars on the road witnessing the incredible event. There were two cars up ahead of them, closer to the object, and there was a car trailing some distance behind them. All of these carloads of people must have seen the craft, but none of them were inclined to stop. The other motorists simply passed the UFO by and went on their way.

The craft now began to exhibit an even stranger phenomenon. A brightly illuminated door of sorts began to materialize on the side of the craft. The opening began as just one small dot of light, but then expanded to trace out an entire door on the ship's hull. Thoroughly in shock at this point, Peter brought the car to a stop as he continued to stare at the object. His paralysis was broken only when he saw that his wife was actually trying to get out of the car!

Sandra later explained that she felt a strange kind of compulsion to walk toward the craft. She opened the car door to go, and only her husband's valiant effort to hold her in place kept her from leaving. The next thing the Taylors recall is taking off at a high rate of speed, barreling on down the road and leaving the object behind. With the strange UFO safely in their rearview mirror, they agreed to simply forget about the whole thing.

The very next day, however, the couple had their first encounter with the Men in Black. These MIB came in the guise of police officers whom the Taylors found waiting for them in a squad car in the driveway of their home. There was no reason for them to be there, no one had called the police—yet they were parked on the Taylors' private property. When they made eye contact, one of the men immediately shouted at them, "Have you anything to report?"

Peter and Sandra supposed that the policeman was referring to the UFO sighting of the day before, but they had already agreed not to talk about the event, so they both responded in the negative. This particular "officer" just wouldn't take no for an answer, however. He continued questioning them, demanding to know what they were doing, where they had been, and why were they were coming home so late. Since they hadn't committed any crime, receiving the third degree from a random police officer was extremely unsettling, but eventually they managed to make their way past the strange figure and on into the safety of their home.

The officer's behavior was aggressive and highly unusual, but that doesn't necessarily mean he was an MIB; bad cops are everywhere, after all. At any rate, the next day Sandra had a drastic change of heart. Deciding that she did want to tell her story, she called up the police department herself, and it wasn't very long at all before two officers showed up at the Taylors' door. In fact, the speed with which they arrived was a bit unusual, since the nearest police station was several miles away.

Adding to the strangeness was the fact that these officers seemed to know all about the incident before Peter or Sandra even explained it to them. The men even volunteered the one kernel of information that Peter and Sandra figured they wouldn't know. They asked, "Other cars were there, weren't they?" After a few more questions, the men informed them that the local police had already thoroughly investigated the matter and determined that what the Taylors had seen was nothing more than a large tent! You can only imagine the couple's reaction as they were told that their life-changing encounter with a UFO was nothing more than a large circus tent pitched on the ground.

After providing this "explanation" for the encounter, one of the officers asked, "Do you want to change your story in light of that?"

To which Sandra emphatically replied, "I am not blind! I have very good eyesight, and I know what I saw!"

The two cops then basically told them, "Very well," and went on their way.

Sandra and Peter thought that this would be the end of it, but to their dumbfounded amazement, a week later they saw a newspaper with the headline "Couple Flees in Terror!" It was a story about the UFO they had witnessed, and Sandra and Peter assumed that the source must be one of the other motorists who were on the road that night. It certainly couldn't have been from them—they thought—since they had declined to even file a report. But incredibly, as they read the paper, they realized that the story was indeed about them! The policemen they had spoken to had apparently leaked their account to the press without their permission.

This unauthorized version of events led to the Taylor home being overwhelmed by all manner of media and UFO enthusiasts, and among this group came an even less desirable element—the Men in Black. As on so many other occasions, these mysterious men arrived in an all-black Cadillac. They wore the standard dark dress of the MIB, and they were also ready to display impressive-looking but ultimately fake IDs that said they were from Great Britain's Ministry of Defense. These men corralled Peter in an isolated room of the house, away from the glare of the cameras, where they sternly told him, "Look, it is in your interests that you do not talk to anyone about this experience." The MIB were once again exerting pressure to shut down the story.

Interestingly enough, this time their targets couldn't agree more. Peter informed the MIB that he would indeed like to keep quiet, but with the intrusive media it was next to impossible. The MIB then offered the simple response, "Leave that to me." To the Taylors' amazement, the man then went out to the throng of reporters and asked them to go somewhere else. Incredibly, the crowd actually listened, and they began to disperse as if they were completely under this entity's control.

Once everyone else was gone, the MIB came back inside and began to interrogate Peter about what he knew about the UFO. He seemed to be especially interested in the door that had appeared on the side of the craft, asking Peter about that one aspect of the event over and over. But Peter, grateful that he'd gotten the news media off his back, was happy to answer as many questions as the Man in Black wanted to ask!

The modus operandi of the MIB silencers was a bit different in the extraordinarily strange case of Dr. Herbert Hopkins. Dr. Hopkins, a UFO investigator and practicing hypnotherapist, was accosted by an MIB in September of 1976. He had been working very hard with a patient from Maine to hammer out the details of the client's experience with UFOs. This work, however, would come to a screeching halt after Dr. Hopkins's brush with the Men in Black.

It all began with a phone call. His wife and kids had left for the afternoon, and almost as soon as he was by himself, his phone began to ring. The person on the other end claimed to be a UFO investigator from New Jersey who had been referred to Dr. Hopkins through fellow investigators. He asked to meet with him to share notes and discuss some of the cases that he had been working on. Dr. Hopkins saw no reason to refuse, and they set up a time for the man to come over later that evening. But it turned out that the man was ready to come sooner than that. In fact, just after Dr. Hopkins hung up the phone and turned on an outside light to help the visitor locate his door, he looked out the window to see a figure clad all in black standing on his doorstep.

As he soon learned, this was the man with whom Dr. Hopkins had just spoken on the phone. Dr. Hopkins would later marvel at the impossibility of the situation. This was long before cellphones, and there were no nearby payphones, so how the man could have been on the phone with him one minute, and then right at his door the next, was a perplexing mystery. Despite the oddness of this arrival, Dr. Hopkins found himself in the full throes of the Oz Factor, and regardless of the strangeness, he readily admitted the man into his home.

Even though Dr. Hopkins's own fears had been paranormally mollified, the same could not be said about his dog, which immediately sensed that something was gravely amiss about the stranger. As soon as the man stepped through the door, the dog barked, whined, and ran off into a closet to hide with its tail between its legs.

As the visitor sat down in his living room, Dr. Hopkins took note of his exact appearance. He was sporting a neatly pressed, and starched, white dress-shirt tucked into black dress pants, with a black tie, and a black suit coat on top. He was also wearing the classic black fedora that the MIB are known for. But it was when the figure took off this hat that his appearance became truly unsettling. As the fedora came off, Dr. Hopkins could see that the man was as pale as death and completely devoid of hair. He was bald, with no facial hair, eyebrows, or even eyelashes. There didn't seem to be one hair on his body. The other odd thing about his appearance was his lips, which were bright cherry red.

Later on, during the course of their conversation, Dr. Hopkins was shocked to watch this MIB wipe his lips with his hand—only to see the lips smudge as if they were nothing more than painted-on makeup! As disconcerting as all of these things were, Dr. Hopkins never considered terminating the interview with the man; he felt that he had to continue answering his questions.

Thus it was the MIB who finally closed out the session, by making the bizarre observation that Dr. Hopkins had "two coins" in his pocket—and then having him check to verify it. Dr. Hopkins dutifully fished in his pocket and reported that there were indeed two coins there. Increasingly feeling like he was being subjected to some odd round of magic tricks, Dr. Hopkins was then instructed to take one of the coins out of his pocket and hold it out in the palm of his hand. His strange visitor then directed him to look carefully at the coin, and to Dr. Hopkins's astonishment, it began to change shape and color in his hand. It was as if the coin was undergoing some sort of spontaneous molecular changes. The coin then suddenly winked out of existence as if it had never been there in the first place.

As Dr. Hopkins stared at his now empty hand in increasing alarm, the MIB flatly informed him, "That coin will never be seen on this planet again." Bizarrely shifting the subject matter, the MIB then asked Dr. Hopkins very seriously if he had ever heard of Barney Hill. He had: Hill was an alien abductee who along with his wife Betty had become one of the most famous cases in ufology. Thinking that the man wanted to compare the facts in the famous case with some of the other cases they had discussed that night, Dr. Hopkins responded that yes, he had heard of Barney, but thought the famed abductee had died recently.

His strange visitor nodded and informed Dr. Hopkins that his recollection was accurate. He then made the cryptic remark that Barney had died because he "didn't have a heart"—and added chillingly, "Just like you no longer have a coin, Barney no longer has a heart." According to the official record, Barney Hill had died of a cerebral aneurism, but this entity seemed to be asserting that his heart had been nullified as easily as the coin—a disturbing suggestion, to say the least!

Immediately after this sinister and threatening insinuation, the MIB ordered Dr. Hopkins to stop talking about UFOs and destroy any information related to his current case. With his mission of threatening and harassing Dr. Hopkins complete, the being then abruptly stood up, and in now oddly faltering speech, announced that his "energy" was "running low". He then bid Dr. Hopkins adieu as he laboriously struggled to get himself out the door.

Dr. Hopkins watched as the man walked down his driveway toward a bright blue light emanating from somewhere in the distance. Then suddenly the light, and the man, were both simply gone—vanished into thin air. Dr. Hopkins was so shaken by the encounter that he immediately destroyed all of his notes on the UFO cases he was working on and refused to even speak of the incident for several years. He became yet another silent witness to the MIB.

The Infallibility of the MIB

The MIB accounts we have related so far in this book are from yesteryear, but rest assured, MIB encounters have continued through the subsequent decades of the 1980s, 1990s, 2000s, and 2010s. One of the most interesting of these more modern meetings occurred on December 1, 1987, when a British policeman named Philip Spencer displayed dogged determination that managed to test the supposed infallibility of the Men in Black.

Spencer was up early that morning, walking through a rural area known as Ilkley Moor, when he received the fright of his life. He saw in the distance an alien being, with greenish skin, an oversized head, and other obviously alien features. As he stared at the entity, it raised a hand as if to motion for him to come forward. In the midst of this adrenalin-inducing encounter, Spencer had the presence of mind to pull out his camera and snap off a quick photo of the being. The entity was apparently camera shy, for as soon as the camera flash went off, the creature took off, running around a large rock outcropping and out of sight. Spencer pursued it, coming to a clearing just in time to see a classic flying saucer-type craft rise off the ground and take off for the horizon at terrific speed.

Spencer then contacted local UFO investigators and presented his evidence of alien contact, so of course it was now just a matter of time before the MIB came calling. The first visit Spencer received from the Men in Black occurred on January 15, 1988. As is common for MIB encounters in England, the men claimed to be from the Ministry of Defense.

They interviewed Spencer about his encounter over the course of the next hour, and it wasn't long before they began to ask about the photograph he had taken. They also requested that Spencer hand over the negative. But Spencer refused, informing the MIB that it had been left with a friend for safekeeping. In reality it was in the hands of UFO investigator Peter Hough.

In this case, if the MIB wished to stop the proliferation of this now infamous photograph, they were already too late. Perhaps the MIB and the dragnet that they attempt to place over all major UFO sightings are not as infallible as they would have us believe. And apparently, it is even possible for pictures and footage of themselves to leak out through the gaps in their blockade.

In recent years, a pair of MIB appear to have been captured on surveillance footage. The incident occurred in 2012 at a hotel in Niagara Falls, Canada, after employees sighted a large triangular UFO. It was the perfect pretext for an MIB encounter, and soon enough two mysterious men, dressed from head to toe in classic Men in Black attire, stormed up to the front desk and began aggressively rattling off questions at the staff.

Like some irate customers just arrived from another dimension, the two MIB demanded to see the hotel manager. As the hotel staff took in the details of the "men" before them, they became increasingly unnerved. Besides the fact that the gentlemen exuded an aura of fear and uneasiness, their general appearance was very strange indeed. They were both very pale, with no hair on their bodies whatsoever, both very tall, and they were seemingly the same exact height. Their faces looked as if they were twins—or maybe clones.

As the staff was scrambling to get ahold of their manager, the men began to babble nearly incoherent nonsense about the government and UFO conspiracies, making a decidedly strange situation even stranger. The uneasy staff, when not subjected directly to the men's lunatic questioning, tried their best to avert their eyes from the MIB's stony gaze. According to them, the men "didn't even blink" and seemed as if they could "look right into one's soul".

Indeed, the staff had the completely disconcerting feeling that these men could actually read their very thoughts! One of the receptionists relates that she actively attempted to change her thoughts while dealing with these unusual visitors, trying her best to "think about something else" so that the MIB wouldn't know what was on her mind! Just imagine this terrified receptionist seated at a desk before these odd men, humming nervously and running through her mind the words, "Think happy thoughts! Just think happy thoughts!"

It's definitely something straight out of the twilight zone, and we would all probably be tempted to believe it never happened in the first place. But when it comes to this crazy story, there is evidence! For whatever reason, the MIB slipped up and allowed themselves to be captured on video. The whole bizarre affair has been forever recorded on the hotel's security cameras. The hotel footage has subsequently been posted online and gone viral.

Fortunately, the MIB, as they sit back in their 1950s Cadillacs, still haven't figured out how to remove content from YouTube! Ever since the release of this strange footage, it has been the object of much speculation for conspiracy theorists all over the globe. If those individuals inside that hotel lobby were indeed members of the infamous Men in Black, they allowed a real gem to slip through their long, thin fingers. If this is the case, it would appear that whoever the MIB are, they are not completely infallible after all.

Who Are the MIB?
And What Do They Want?

So, who exactly are the MIB, and what do they want from an unsuspecting humanity? This one sentence sums up the ultimate end goal of decades worth of investigation into the Men in Black. But these two fundamental questions still remain largely unanswered.

Gray Barker was the first to put the spotlight on the phenomenon back in the 1950s with his book *They Knew Too Much About Flying Saucers*. Barker believed that the men were nothing more than government agents who were hell-bent upon repressing the truth about UFOs. But as this book demonstrated, important branches of the U.S. government such as the Air Force, CIA, and FBI have indicated that they know nothing at all about these mysterious individuals. Their own internal memoranda seem to substantiate these denials. The release of these previously top-secret memos years after the fact indicates that the U.S. government was just as eager as anyone else to figure out who these men were.

This eagerness was on full display in the infamous case of Rex Heflin. After Heflin indicated that Air Force imposters had visited him, a direct order went out to all members of the USAF that anyone who witnessed or even heard mention of these strange happenings should immediately report to Air Force intelligence. This would seem to clearly indicate that much of the U.S. government was in the dark as to just who the MIB were.

Albert Bender was one of the first subjects of MIB activity, and he was also the one who first posited the theory that these beings were not agents from any Earthly government but were actually alien beings from another planet. John Keel partially concurred with this theory in the 1960s after his episodes with the Mothman in West Virginia. But he believed that the beings were not so much from another planet as from another dimension—which is why he coined the term "ultra-terrestrial" in regard to the phenomenon.

Others have continued to expand upon the theory that the MIB come from beyond. They are claimed to be everything from time travelers to some strange manifestation of our collective consciousness itself.

One common attribute of these MIB is the fact that they always seem to be one step ahead of us—especially when it comes to the targets of their harassment. They seem to know an astounding number of intimate details about the people they choose to visit, indeed, even their very thoughts! But as much as they know about us, we know next to nothing about them—and it seems that the MIB—whoever they are—are very much content to keep it that way.

Further Readings

Let's now take a quick look at some of the many resources that helped to make this book on the MIB possible. Here you will find a wide variety of data on the phenomenon of the Men in Black, spanning several decades. If you would like to know more about the complex nature of the Men in Black phenomenon, then feel free to browse through these sources of MIB information as well.

***They Knew Too Much About Flying Saucers.* Gray Barker**
This is a classic book dating all the way back to the 1950s. It's set in the aftermath of Albert Bender's abrupt resignation from the IFSB. Investigative journalist and UFO pioneer Gray Barker crafts an interesting tale of mystery and intrigue as he tries to determine just who is trying to put the lid on research into UFOs. Barker had his own run-ins with an MIB, and he believed that the recent shutdown of his friend Bender's UFO investigation team, the IFSB, was also due to pressure from these mysterious figures. Barker always thought that the MIB were nothing more than government agents, however, and expresses as much in the book.

***Flying Saucers and the Three Men.* Albert Bender**
This was the book that Albert Bender, the previous head of the silenced UFO group, the IFSB, wrote to finally shed some light on what had happened to him. His story depicts the same mysterious agents that Gray Barker described nearly a decade before, but Bender casts a much more supernatural light on these beings. Indeed, he soon reveals his belief that the MIB are nothing short of extraterrestrial creatures attempting to cover their own tracks!

Gray Barker, who always insisted that the MIB were fully human, was quite upset with this book's conclusion, and even went so far as to tell fellow UFO buffs not to believe it. Barker even insinuated that Bender had created his fantastical tale as disinformation—perhaps even at the behest of the MIB themselves. This was allegedly an effort to steer people away from what was really happening. Fact, fiction, or fantasy, it still makes for an interesting read.

The Truth Behind the Men in Black. Jenny Randles

This book, written by Jenny Randles, a celebrated UFO investigator from across the pond, remains a tremendous resource for anyone seeking to know more about the international aspect of MIB. In particular, Randles provides great insight into the British MIB encounters. Her book is a great supplement to what is already known about the U.S. based phenomenon, helping to provide detail on what is in fact a wider ranging, international occurrence.

World Encyclopedia of UFO and Alien Encounters

This book is an absolutely great resource when it comes to all things UFO and aliens, and it provides a great reference point for MIB encounters as well. If you would like to know more about many of the events described in this book, as well as other cases not mentioned here, read this book.

The Real Men in Black. Nick Redfern

Nick Redfern has long been an MIB enthusiast and has spent many years researching reports of the Men in Black. This book provides a wide range of insights into the phenomenon. If you would like to know more about the MIB, then you should most definitely get a copy of this book!

The Crack in the Universe. **Jean-Claude Bourret**
For anyone interested in the metaphysical aspect of MIB, this book provides a true wealth of data and viewpoints on the subject. If you would like to know more about the inter-dimensional nature often ascribed to MIB activity, then you are going to want to read this book as well!

www.mysteriousuniverse.com
Mysterious Universe has articles on all manner of things paranormal, and it has plenty of info on the MIB as well. The aforementioned Nick Redfern is one of the frequent contributors for Mysterious Universe, and the insight that he provides is second to none.

Also by Conrad Bauer

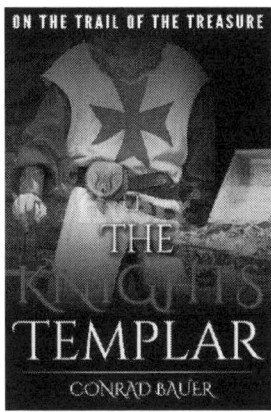

Made in United States
Orlando, FL
26 May 2024